Why Must I..

Wash my Hands?

Jackie Gaff

**Photography by
Chris Fairclough**

CHERRYTREE BOOKS

A Cherrytree book

First published in 2005 by
Evans Brothers Ltd
2A Portman Mansions
Chiltern Street
London W1U 6NR

VISIT OUR WEBSITE
www.evansbooks.co.uk
Evans

British Library Cataloguing in Publication Data
Gaff, Jackie
   Why Must I wash my hands?
   1.Hand washing – Juvenile literature 2.Hygiene – Juvenile literature
   I.Title
   613.4

ISBN 1–84234259–2

Planned and produced by Discovery Books Ltd
Editor: Helena Attlee
Designer: Ian Winton
Illustrator: Joanna Williams
Consultant: Pat Jackson, Professional Officer for School Nursing, The Community Practitioners' and
Health Visitors' Association.

Acknowledgements

The author and publisher would like to thank the following for kind permission to reproduce photographs:
Corbis: p8 right (Ron Boardman/FLPA/Corbis), p25 bottom (David Thomas/Picture Arts/Corbis); Getty
Images: p9 bottom (Stone), p16 bottom (Stone); Science Photo Library: p8 left (Sinclair Stammers/SPL),
p20 top (WG/SPL); David Simson: p7 top.
Commissioned photography by Chris Fairclough.

The author, packager and publisher would like to thank the following people for their participation in
the book: Alice Baldwin-Hay, Heather, Charlotte and William Cooper, Ieuan Crowe, Caitlin and Rosabel
Hudson, and the staff and pupils of Presteigne County Primary School.

Contents

Why must I wash my hands?

Washing your hands with soap and water makes them clean, but do you know why dirty hands can be harmful?

It is bad for you to have dirt on your hands, because **germs** love it. If you have germs on your hands, they can easily get into your mouth, eyes or nose.

Your hands might look clean, but they could still be covered in germs.

To wash your hands properly, wet them in warm water. Now rub soap on to the front and back, between your fingers and around your wrists.

Once germs get inside your body, they can give you anything from a cold to an upset stomach.

Germs are so small that you can't see them. That's why washing your hands is so important.

HEALTHY HINTS

- **Remember that germs hate soap and water.**
- **Always scrub your hands well after you use the toilet.**
  - **Don't forget to wash your thumbs.**
  - **Don't forget to wash after playing outside.**

Always wash before you touch food. You don't want to eat germs for tea!

How does soap work?

Soap is made up of tiny units called molecules.
Soap molecules are attracted to dirt.

Soap **molecules** break dirt down into tiny specks.
Then they surround each speck of dirt.

Once they are surrounded
by soap molecules, the
dirt specks can't
stick to your
skin any more.

You don't always need a bath or shower to keep clean - just soap and water!

Ancient soap

Soap was invented about 4,000 years ago. The first soap was made from wood ash, oil and clay. How would you like to wash your hands in oil and ash?

When you rinse your hands, the clean water washes the soap and dirt specks away – along with any germs that were hitching a ride in the dirt.

What are germs?

There are thousands of different kinds of germs. Some of them are so tiny that millions could fit on this full stop.

The smallest germs are called **viruses**. They cause many different illnesses. For example, colds and **chicken pox** are both caused by viruses.

Germs are tiny living things that can only be seen under a microscope.

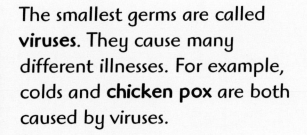

This is what a flu virus looks like under a microscope.

Bacteria are another group of germs. Some of them give you earache, and others cause a sore throat.

There are also lots of helpful bacteria. Scientists use these to make medicines.

Harmful germs can only make you sick if they get inside you. So wage war on germs – wash your hands!

HEALTHY HINTS

- **Treat germs mean – stay clean!**
- **Do not put dirty fingers in your eyes, nose or mouth.**

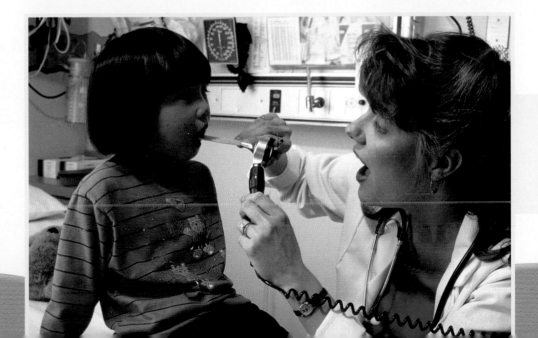

If you do get sick, you may need to see a doctor.

Germ warfare

Don't worry, your body is brilliant at fighting off harmful germs.

Your skin stops most germs from getting inside your body. Tears wash away germs from your eyes, and nose hairs trap germs too.

Unfortunately, harmful germs sometimes get past all your body barriers. Then they **multiply**, making more and more of themselves.

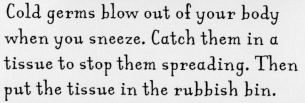

Cold germs blow out of your body when you sneeze. Catch them in a tissue to stop them spreading. Then put the tissue in the rubbish bin.

Germs can make you ill. They might make your nose run, or give you a **rash** or a **fever**. Luckily, there are special fighting **cells** in your blood that kill off germs.

Remember it's easy to spread germs when you are ill. Stop them in their tracks, clean up your act!

Wash your hands after visiting a sick friend.

Cuts and grazes

If you cut or graze your skin, your blood rushes to the rescue.

Wounds bleed so that the special fighting cells in your blood can kill off any germs.

Bad cuts or grazes may need covering with a plaster or bandage to keep dirt and germs out.

Other blood cells also get to work, lumping and clumping together to make a **scab**.

Help your body. Always ask an adult to clean a wound and put a plaster on if you need one.

The scab's job is to plug the gap in your skin and keep germs out. When new skin grows to heal the cut, the scab will fall off.

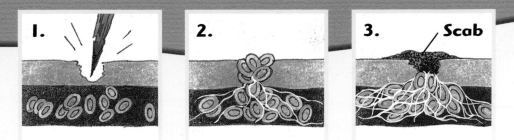

1. If you cut yourself, it gives germs the chance to enter your body. 2. Red blood cells block the wound. 3. A scab forms.

If you pick a scab off before it's ready, you can open the cut *again*. The cut will take longer to heal and you may even get a **scar**.

HEALTHY HINTS

- **Wash your hands with soap before touching a wound.**

- **Try not to pick at scabs.**

- **Beware! Some people are allergic to plasters.**

Smelly stuff

Soap and water don't just lift dirt from your skin. They also clean away smelly sweat, oil and dead skin.

Sweating is your body's way of cooling itself down. As sweat dries on your skin it allows your body to lose heat, and this makes you feel cooler and more comfortable.

Sweat comes out of tiny holes in your skin called pores.

When sweat dries on clothes it makes them smelly, too. Keep your kit clean!

Sweat does not smell too bad when it's fresh. But if you don't wash the sweat off, bacteria starts to feed on it, and then things get smelly.

There are no prizes for guessing the best way to keep smells at bay – soap and water, of course!

HEALTHY HINTS

- **Wash well – don't smell.**
- **Put dirty clothes in the wash.**

Bath-time

So now you know why you have to get wet all over – your hands aren't the only body bits that get dirty!

Having a bath or a shower is the best way to keep your whole body clean and healthy.

Start washing at the top, with your face, neck and ears. Then work your way down to your toes.

Toys and sweet-smelling bubbles can make bath-time a real treat.

Make sure you give a good wash to the places where dirt and germs really like to collect – under your arms and between your legs.

HEALTHY HINTS

- **Try to have a bath or a shower every day.**
- **Wash and dry yourself carefully from head to toe.**
- **Shower after you swim, or the chlorine in the pool can make your skin itch.**

Dry yourself all over with a soft, clean towel.

I hate hair-washing!

Yes, you hate washing your hair, but doesn't it look, feel and smell fabulous after the washing, rinsing and combing is all over!

Dirty hair looks dull and oily. It also makes your head itchy and smelly, because bacteria are feasting on the dirt, oil and dead skin.

Rub your scalp and hair gently with your fingertips. Rinse until the water runs clear.

Some people have dry hair, and others have oily hair. Whatever kind of hair you have, wash it with shampoo at least once a week. This will keep it clean and sweet smelling.

Unbrushed hair is full of messy tangles and knots. Try to brush it as often as you can.

Conditioner helps to make your hair shiny and tangle-free. Comb it through your hair with a wide-toothed comb.

HEALTHY HINTS

- Comb or brush your hair every day when you get up.

- Wash your hair at least once a week.

- Choose a shampoo or conditioner to suit your hair type.

- Wash your brush and comb to keep them clean.

19

Not so nice lice

It isn't fair. Keeping your hair clean doesn't stop bugs from setting up home on your head.

Head lice aren't picky. They love all kinds of hair – long or short, dirty or clean.

This is a magnified picture. Head lice are really no bigger than a pin head, and nits are even smaller.

Lice feed by sucking your blood, and they lay their eggs on your hair. Head lice eggs are called nits.

Don't worry, there are special lotions for killing lice, and combs for getting rid of nits.

It's hard to spot lice and nits because they are so small. Their bites are very itchy though, so that is what you need to watch out for.

Stop lice spreading – never borrow or lend hats, headphones, brushes or combs.

HEALTHY HINTS

- **Ask an adult to check your hair each week for any signs of head lice.**

- **Brush or comb your hair often as this puts head lice off.**

- **Don't panic – lice and nits can be zapped.**

Fingers and toes

What do your nails look like? Are they neat, or are they cracked and torn? Are the tips clean, or are they grubby?

The tips of your nails are real dirt traps. Try to pay special attention to them when you wash your hands. Use a soft nailbrush if they are very grubby.

Cracked and torn nails let germs under your skin, just as cuts and grazes do.

Keep your nails neatly trimmed and don't nibble them.

HEALTHY HINTS

- **Trim your nails after a shower or bath, when they're clean and slightly softer.**

- **Tell an adult if your feet are sore.**

- **Change your socks often.**

Germs invade your mouth as well as your skin when you bite your nails.

Sweaty feet aren't just smelly, they feed the germs that cause **athlete's foot**. This is a skin disease that makes the skin between the toes itchy, flaky and sore.

Wash and dry your feet carefully, especially between your toes.

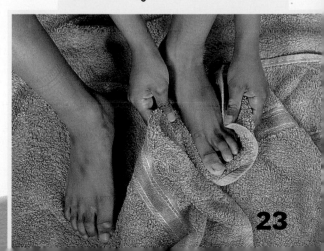

23

Kitchen safety

Germs are greedy. They feast on anything they can find, including the food in your kitchen.

When germs get to work, they make food rot. Eating bad food can make you very sick.

Frighten germs away by keeping the kitchen clean. Wash the dishes, wipe the surfaces, and always wash your hands before you touch food.

Cooking is fun, but always ask an adult for help.

Be sure to wash raw vegetables and fruit before you start munching.

Germs love the food we get from animals. This means everything from milk, cheese and eggs to fish, chicken, beef and other meats. Never eat uncooked eggs, fish or meat.

HEALTHY HINTS

- **Wash hands before eating, and before and after preparing food.**

- **Always use warm water and soap.**

- **Never eat food that looks or smells bad.**

Fish and meat must be cooked carefully, so that they are hot all the way through.

Pet care

Pets can give you heaps of love and hours of fun, but they can also spread disease. Stay safe, not sorry!

All animals can spread bugs or germs. It doesn't mean that you have to stop loving them. It does mean that you need to take care around them.

Don't kiss your pet, and try not to let it lick you. Make sure you wash your hands after touching a pet or its food.

Love your pets, but don't catch their germs. Wash your hands after playing with them.

Never touch animal droppings. If you touch them by accident, make sure you give your hands a good scrub with warm water and soap.

Always tell an adult if a pet or other animal bites or scratches you.

Wash your hands very carefully after cleaning out a pet cage.

Stay clean, stay healthy

Now you know why everyone is always on at you to wash! Staying clean is the best way to keep your body healthy and happy.

You'd have to be very unlucky to catch a really nasty **disease**, but everyone gets colds.

Germs can spread through the air in coughs and sneezes – one sneeze can blast them as far as 10 metres!

Germs also spread by touch. One of the quickest ways to catch a cold is by rubbing your nose or eyes when your hands have cold germs on them.

Healthy bodies have fun –
they don't lie in bed feeling
sick and sorry.

Soap and water are your weapon in
the war against germs that could
make you sick. They also stop you
spreading germs that could make
other people ill.

So, when was the last time you
washed your hands?

HEALTHY HINTS

- **Take care not to catch germs.**

- **Take care not to spread germs to others.**

- **Keep your whole body clean, not just your hands.**

Glossary

Athlete's foot
A skin disease that makes skin between the toes and on the soles of the feet itchy and scaly.

Bacteria
Bacteria are tiny, single-celled living things.

Cell
Cells are the body's building blocks, just as bricks are a house's building blocks. Every part of you is made up of its own kinds of cells.

Chicken pox
A disease that causes a fever and an itchy rash of dark red spots. The spots turn into blisters, then scabs which eventually drop off.

Disease
Another word for an illness or sickness.

Fever
An illness which makes your body temperature rise above its normal level of about 37°C.

Germ
A tiny living thing that causes disease.

Molecule
Molecules are one of the basic units of matter.

Multiply
To increase in number, or make more of.

Rash
A number of tiny spots on the skin.

Scab
A scab is the hard crust of dried blood that forms over a wound to protect it while it heals.

Scar
A scar is a mark that is sometimes left on the skin after a wound heals and the scab falls off.

Sweat
Sweat is salty liquid produced by your skin to get rid of waste materials and to help it cool down. As it dries on your skin, sweat makes you feel cooler.

Virus
A microscopic living thing that can cause diseases.

Wound
Bruises, burns, cuts and grazes are all wounds.

Further resources

Websites

www.bbc.co.uk/health
BBC website containing articles and news on all aspects of child and adult health.

www.canandianparents.com
A lively website covering all aspects of family life, including health and hygiene.

www.everybody.co.nz
New Zealand's health information website.

www.gphealthsmart.com
A general health site, including materials for teaching children about general and personal hygiene.

www.kidshealth.org
American, child-centred site devoted to all aspects of health and wellbeing. Includes advice on hand washing, skincare and general hygiene.

Books

At Home With Science: Splish! Splosh! Why Do We Wash?, Janice Lobb, Kingfisher, 2002.

Look After Yourself:Healthy Hair, Angela Royston, Heinemann Library, 2003.

Look After Yourself: Healthy Skin, Angela Royston, Heinemann Library, 2003.

My Amazing Body: Staying Healthy, Angela Royston, Raintree, 2004.

Your Body, Claire Llewellyn, Franklin Watts, 2002.

Your Hair, Claire Llewellyn, Franklin Watts, 2002.

Index